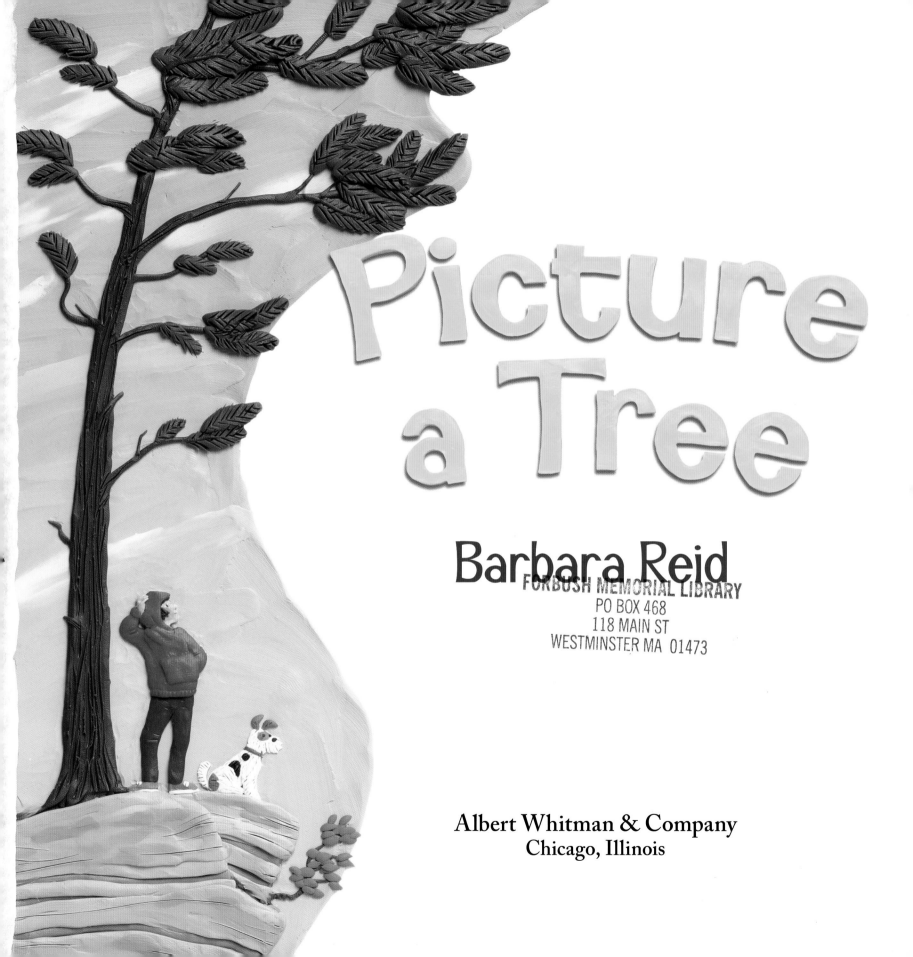

Picture a Tree

Barbara Reid

Albert Whitman & Company
Chicago, Illinois

The illustrations in this book were made with Plasticine that
was shaped and pressed onto illustration board.
Paint was used for special effects.

The type is set in Adobe Caslon Pro.

Photography by Ian Crysler.

Library of Congress Cataloging-in-Publication Data

Reid, Barbara.

Picture a tree / Barbara Reid.

p. cm.

Summary: "Explores in words and pictures
different ways of seeing and experiencing trees"—Provided by publisher.

ISBN 978-0-8075-6526-1 (hardcover)

[1. Trees—Fiction.] I. Title.

PZ7.R2646Pi 2013

[E]—dc23

2012019530

For more information about Albert Whitman & Company,
visit our web site at www.albertwhitman.com.

To Ruby

There is more than one
way to picture a tree.

You may see a drawing on the sky.

A game of dress-up.

The first drops
of color . . .

then all the art
supplies at once.

A tunnel

or an ocean.

A tree can be
a high-rise
home sweet home.

A pirate ship,

a bear cave,

a clubhouse,

a friend.

Some trees are sun umbrellas

on the hot walk home.

There are baby trees,

in-betweens,

grown-ups,

grandfathers.

You may see the end of
one thing, or the start of
something new.

A wild good-bye party.

A glow in the
darkness . . .

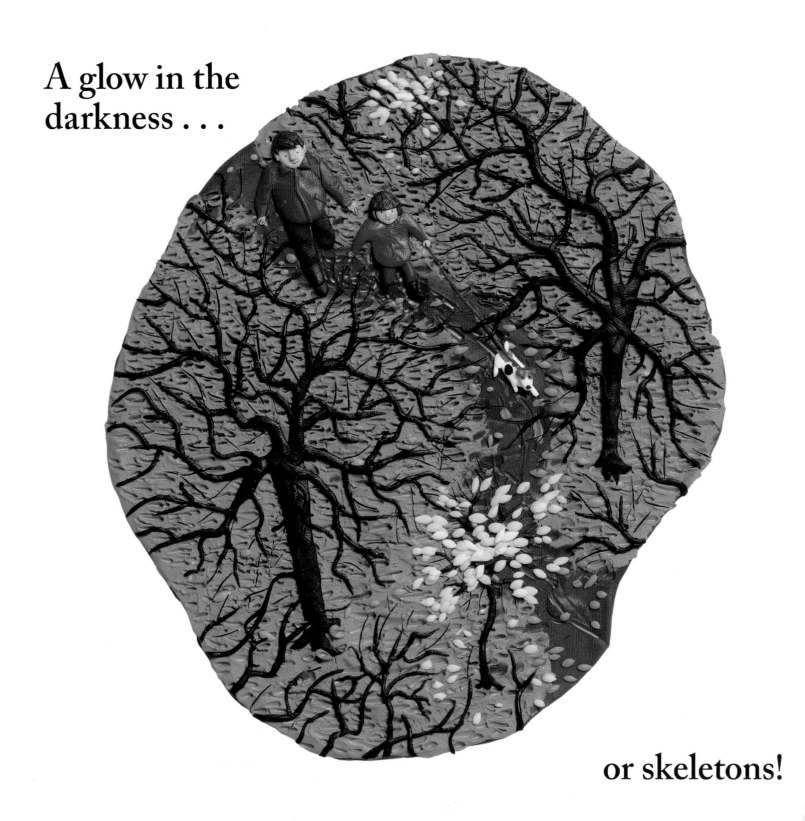

or skeletons!

Some trees put on snowsuits.

28

Every winter tree holds spring,

sleeping like a baby.

Picture a tree. What do *you* see?